"Mind Your Own Damn Business"

Life Brings Many Challenges And
Sometime You're Not Prepared
For What It Throws At You

Annette E. Riley Joseph

"Mind Your Own Damn Business"

Life Brings Many Challenges And Sometime
You're Not Prepared
For What It Throws At You

By Annette E. Riley Joseph

©2010, 2016

Published in the United States of America

All rights reserved.

M.O.R.E. Publishers CO
Memphis, Tennessee
https://MOREPublishers.biz/
www.TheScaleMagazine.MagCloud.com

COVER PHOTO BY ANNETTE JOSEPH

ISBN: 978-1-945344-01-5

INTRODUCTION

Life changes in front of your eyes. I try to find the girl I used to be, but as I get older, it's harder to find her. She was surrounded by friends and family who loved her and all she wanted to do was disappear.

It was as if she was trying to find a lost person. With her hair pressed and curled and her green sundress, she still felt ugly. So, she tried to cover up in jeans and a sweatshirt, but she had to take a family picture.

Why is it so hard for girls to accept themselves? I'll tell you why. It's because our bodies change on us so much. Some girls accept it, but most girls don't. Some girls make small things a big deal, like having a boyfriend. But heartache comes with that.

It's tough to be a woman, especially when everyone, but you, don't play by all the rules. It's hard to look in the mirror and not see the real you. It's like you fade away and you turn into someone else.

Where there was once an eternal smile on your face, now lies an unattractive badge of unhappiness, and you can't do anything about it because that's life.

I look at the TV and observe all of the crime and the killing, and sometimes it brings tears to my eyes. When I see people with dirty clothes on their backs, I see what life has done to them.

People drink, or take pills and sometimes they don't know when to say "no" to anything. It's because they have no salvation.

Salvation saves you from danger. When you look into the mirror, you see a scared child who doesn't know how to deal with pressure. Well, salvation saves him too.

People say they that they wish that they were kids again. They think that they have all of the answers in life, but they are wrong.

You struggle to keep yourself together in life no matter what age. Some people never complain, but some people say that they never have enough. Salvation makes people strong. Happiness doesn't come from material things. It comes from having peace in the mind. This is what you call salvation.

People try to make reasons why they are content with life, but they are just trying to please everyone.

Remember, it's their life, not yours. "Mind Your Own Damn Business." Life brings many challenges and sometimes you're not prepared for what it throws at you. Are you prepared for everything that is going to come your way?

RATIONALE

The reason I'm writing this is because I have people ask me every day where my front teeth are.

I brush and take care of them, but I still get asked this question. Then when I go to the nursing home, the interrogations cease. I use my hands and feet to work, not my teeth to talk.

People always talk about appearances. They never accept others for who they are. It's not your responsibility to change others.

Stop criticizing others about their teeth, or clothes, or shape. If people were more loving, you probably wouldn't have so many angry people nowadays.

Why do people try to fix you when there's nothing wrong? Words of wisdom would say – get out and do some things. Even I did in my later years. Enjoy.

Author's Note

The reason I wanted the pictures in the book is because my Mother always told her children "Get a little culture in your life".

The places I visited tell my stories. Remember, a lot of people don't get to see the places.

I was in the right place at the right time for me to enjoy the places.

To Angelee

From Annette Joseph

- Introduction 03
- Rationale 05
- Author's Note 06
- Eyes Looking Through A Window 09
- Being Single 10
- Sometimes People Think They're The Only Ones Suffering 11
- Desperate 13
- Wisdom 16
- Happy Birthday 18
- Song 1928
- Silence Is Golden 21
- As Things Get Old, Nothing Ever Changes 23
- Message To Parents Of A Sickly/Disabled Child 25
- Envy 27
- When You Doubt - Fear Enters Your Life 28
- The Visits 35
- Growing Old And Being All Alone 43
- A Precious Thing 45
- Wasting Away 55
- Crush 57
- The Story of Boxes 59
- Sparkles 61

Inside

- Window of Yourself   63
- Damage   65
- Search for Truth   67
- Thrown Away   69
- Life's Changing In Front of Your Eyes   71
- Conclusion: Stop Fighting   77
- Dedication   78
- Other Readings   79
- From the Editor   81

Eyes Looking Through A Window

Have you ever wondered what your eyes see? Well, it's you. Have you ever wondered how many faces you see in the car, the store, on your way to work?

You see the crime on TV and get tired of it and change the channel. Do you wonder how many people cry over it? Do you hate violent playbacks of crime in your mind? I do.

Then you have children who make you happy and who make you smile and you see infants with their jolly smiles. Everything you see isn't always bad. Sometimes you don't want to see drama. You want to see the joy in people's eyes, even it for a split second.

Eyes see so far away. They don't mean to talk to you. But they do. Look through your heart, not your eyes.

Being Single

Being single can be tough, especially when people only think of young, single people. Singles are also people who have lost their mates too. People label everything.

Why do we have to be labeled as people without ANYONE? What's the big deal? What's wrong with being single? Does this word automatically mean that you must be old or that something is wrong with you? I don't think so.

Companions can be friends. One reason that so many people are single is because they use words the wrong way. Some people like being single. There is nothing wrong with it. But no one wants to be alone.

So, go out and meet people because you can't talk to yourself. I understand love is so hard to find. Some people don't know how to love themselves, or other people. You have to have fun. Don't try to fit in where you don't belong.

Take a chance. Look beyond your surroundings. Enjoy your life and if you find love, then great! Don't let labels define you. Remember, you were born single in this world. Don't be so serious. Search your heart for what you want because you never know when you will have your last day on earth.

Sometimes People Think
That They're The Only Ones Suffering

Each and every night, somebody somewhere is hurting. They could be dying from cancer or maybe they had a stroke, and they can't communicate with anyone. There are so many people who are hurting. They have no one to which they can turn.

They don't want everybody to know their business. Loneliness is a hurting thing but we can't do anything about it. Some people just can't fit in with others.

Humans are the evilest beings I have ever seen. They don't know how to treat each other.

You have heard this over and over, and over again – women get cruel men, and men get selfish women, but neither can stay away from each other.

No one knows how to treat each other right. Good people end up with bad people. They lower their standards. What makes them think a person is supposed to act the way they want them to act?

It's a constant struggle if you don't want that person to be honest. People constantly lie to make themselves feel good.

A lot of people bring pain and misery to their life. They don't want people to think they are a failure. But who cares? You're the one hurting.

You are not a failure. It's what's important to you - **NOT** everybody else. The heart does heal however.

Desperate

I look in the sky and it looks like it's on fire. I take a picture, because I want to see it again. I'm sitting on the back porch watching the neighbors take care of their yard. Every time someone opens their mouth, it's all about them. It should really be about who counts their blessings.

A lot of people appreciate what they have. It's the haters who find fault. When you have accomplished tasks, you wanted to do, they want to tear you down. But they can't, because some people are born with goodness in their heart, like Mother Teresa.

Mother Teresa in India

She was mistreated, but she kept going on. Her name is spoken by everyone – no matter what race you are.

Unfortunately, though I have never seen so much hate in this world. No one is trying to stop it – not the police, not even private citizens. Everyone talks a good talk, but no one tries to change anything. Now everything is about drugs, sex, and money.

There are jealous people. They had them in the old days, and they have them now. You see, people love misery. They love having power over their peers. Everyone needs to go back and find out what is important to them in their life.

You can say what you have, but if you no longer have it, then it means nothing. Living life and enjoying life are two totally different things. No one can effectively judge the quality of your lifestyle. Not unless they have going through the exact same things you have gone through and have set and achieved the exact same goals.

You can't let people tear you down. Believe in yourself. Life can be unfair, but you can't let life's problems take over your life. Love yourself and remember that you don't need other people's approval. Take a look at yourself. Find things you love about yourself and make yourself smile. You don't need society's approval to appreciate yourself, which is what is most important. Stop tearing yourself down! God thinks you're special, so you should think the same.

St. Louis Brewery side street (public domain photo)

Wisdom

When you think of wisdom, what comes to your mind? Experience? Challenges? Maybe all of the things you've been through in life up until now. But to me, wisdom is the simple things in life taken for granted. You could just be getting out of bed every morning, then all of a sudden, you can't pay your bills, and you're in the dark. You have no control over that.

Moreover, when your children grow up so fast, you remember a time when you saw them every day. Now, you're lucky to get a phone call or a visit. Wisdom is when you didn't think about things before you did them, and now you regret the decisions you made.

Now maybe you're in a nursing home with a bunch of strangers watching your body waste away. Sometimes you can't even open a jar of jelly, because it's too tight, or you can't even use the can opener. Then when you look in the mirror, you can't even recognize yourself.

The simple things you took for granted – that's wisdom! You may be thinking, well, you can open a jar with someone's help, or you can use an electric can opener. That's not the point. You don't have to be old for these things to happen to you. You have to be on top of your game.

That goes for your body, life, job, and children. You have to be ready for everything life throws at you. If you are not prepared, you will fall on your butt! Remember, some things you can control, but when you can't control something life throws at you, you have to be prepared to deal with it. You are not a child anymore. There are NO EXCUSES!

Photo by Annette Joseph

Happy Birthday

I'm sitting here thinking about my mother. Her birthday just passed. Every year when her birthday comes around, I say "happy birthday" to remember her. She is always in my thoughts.

I wonder if she is proud of her family and what they have done in their lives? People on the street ask me about my mother, and when I tell them that she is dead, they tell me what a nice person she was. That is a good feeling. I will always remember my mother and let everyone know that her birthday was May 4th. She has a lot of family, and on May 4th, everyone will remember my mother.

Happy Birthday Mother,

From all of your descendants

Song

It's amazing how a song can bring good and bad thoughts to your mind. Some songs make you fall into a romantic mood. Others may make you remember the past. Some songs help set the mood. They bring you to tears, or make you have butterflies.

Songs sometime make you lose touch with reality. But you always have to find your way back. Sometimes you can hear a certain tune that may make you think of your first crush, and you wonder if they think about you when they hear the same song, even though life went on after that time.

Next time when you hear a song, I hope it is a good feeling, and not a bad one. No one can take away your memory of the past. But only you can decide what you feel about the past now.

Silence Is Golden

Have you ever wondered why people say silence is golden? People can be so cruel. But when the tables turn, they become angry.

You don't always have to tell people what you think of them. People already know their flaws when they look in the mirror.

Some people hate everything about themselves, and they wish that they weren't ever born. Everyone is born for a reason.

You have to look outside the box. Think about what is important to you in life and do what you want to do. If you want to quit your job, then quit it! You weren't born to that job.

Stop being afraid of yourself. If you worry about what people think, you won't achieve your goals in like.

This is why silence is golden. What's important to one person may not be important to another person.

One of our travels

Stop fighting yourself to survive. You survived your birth, you can survive life. The steps you take in life are a part of the road.

As Things Get Old, Nothing Ever Changes

I was sitting and listening to the news and they were talking about Blacks, elections, and how Blacks vote. I know that some people never vote in their lives. I think that this is wrong.

Black people have faults just like every other race. We don't need to be put in a group. But we don't try to change their opinion of us.

This isn't even important to me. It's a part of dealing with life. I see sickness around me every day. That's what's important to me. Finding a cure for different diseases and treatment for premature babies are important.

People argue about race as their life flashes by. That's not important to me. There are so many other issues to talk about, more importantly, to solve other than race. But this issue is what keeps people going. When diseases are mentioned in the news, race talk is slid into the issue once again. IT DOESN'T MATTER!!!

People don't care about race. People are dying and they only want a cure so they can live longer. These are the very reasons people don't donate their organs. It's because of mistrust. People forget that there are issues like war and kidnapping. People don't do anything to help the situations.

Everybody won't like you no matter – Black or White. Other races don't fight like the Black and White races do. They just move on with life. Remember, all of us are going to die and the next generation will live on. Don't let them be born in hate. When you're in the hospital, does it matter who cares for you? No, as long as you get your care.

You only care about what race is around you when you're independent, and you can defend yourself. In the end, we all need each other no matter what your race. Think about that.

Message To Parents
Of A Sickly/Disabled Child

I know that a lot of you were surprised when you found out the doctor had to tell you that there was something wrong with your child. You're scared and you don't know what to think.

I admire the strength in you for being able to go to the hospital every day, sitting by your child, and not showing how worried you really are. For giving your child the best care and while taking the child home, you became a nurse to your child.

You NEVER thought that this could happen to you or your child. When you have a disabled child, you have people whisper behind your back and tell you what's good for your child. Then you have to put your child in an organization so he/she can learn independently and live on their own, if something should happen to you. No one can walk in your shoes because they don't have the patience that you have as a parent.

A long time ago, having a sick child was looked down upon. People wanted the parent to put them in a nursing home or an institution. Things have changed for the better for these children. They can stay at home with their family. They can even have a job and an apartment with helpers to teach them how to cook, clean, and fit in with society.

I know that you (parents) want to protect your children because they are from you. But they know that you love them. People are watching you parents. You are a source of strength. Have courage. Keep a good heart. Hold onto your faith.

Envy

Never be envious of somebody because you think that their life is better. Life has many surprises. Sometimes we want the wrong things in life. Look inside yourself, and think about what you miss in life. If you only got one parent to raise you, then you're lucky.

Think of the child with parents. Some children are in the system all of their lives because they are never adopted. They don't even know what family is. Some people who you think have it easy actually have it rough in life. Some people have self-pity. They have nothing to complain about. They are never satisfied. Yet they are blessed.

They are angry because they have to work for what they have. There is no easy way in life. You're not in jail or anything. You walk out of your home without a care, and you still envy people. You look at what these people have, but you're not willing to go through what they went through to get what they got.

You are not in a contest. This is your life. If you want a dream to come true, don't just talk about it. Make it happen! Invest in yourself. Don't be envious of what people have whether it is clothes, cars, family, or job. Just open your heart, and take a look inside yourself. You'll find the answer.

St. Louis by Yinin Chin

When You Doubt - Fear Enters Your Life

I was standing outside thinking to myself how people use race against you. I was told that I would never see some of the places that I've been because I'm Black. But that was a lie. If it's in your power to do something, do it.

I was forced to retire because I became sick. I tried to join a program that offered things, but they said that I was too young to join, even though I was in my fifties. I got into another program. Now I see things that I only heard about, or saw on TV.

A day at the races
photo by Annette Joseph

Arcadia Theater

My first trip was the Arcadia Jamboree in Ironton, Missouri. I had never heard of that place before I visited there, even though I've been in St. Louis all of this time.

The show was about impersonating famous people. The food was good. Also, I did not feel out of place because overall, it was a group of seniors having fun.

Anheuser Busch (St. Louis) photo by Annette Joseph

I have also been to the St. Charles Tour. We ate at Miss Aimee B's Restaurant.

I have been to an opera. Then we had dinner at a restaurant. I was born and reared in St. Louis, and I did not know that we had all of these treasures – the plays, and the diversity.

My next trip was the Palace Theatre where the musical American Organ Concert was being held. We even sang songs. This brought back great memories.

I even went to our Lady of the Snow. It was beautiful and after that we went out for dinner.

The next year, I went to a fancy restaurant. Everything was so great. It was like eating at home. Overall, I'm saying that I never thought that I would see the things that I've seen. I've learned so much on these trips. For instance, I didn't know that the Science Center serves breakfast.

I have seen educational movies. I've even seen how plays and stages are put together.

(Keeze – CCC)

My next trip was Grafton.

Eckert's Farm, Belleville (Illinois)

Pick your own apples!

Grafton Auckland Bridge

Pumpkin Farm by Paul Brennan (CCC)

On that trip, we traveled around the city observing the rocks. Then the bus turned into a ferry, which was a new experience for me.

Later, we went to an old-time restaurant. It was as if it was right out of a movie. The waiters served us fried chicken, roast beef, homemade country sausage, and dessert.

My future trips included watching *The Full Monty*. We had lunch in Allandale Brewery in Kirkwood, Missouri, before they closed and are under new management.

I am telling you about these adventures because, instead of sitting alone at home, feeling sorry for myself, I go out and explore my surroundings. Even though I was too young to join a program with pre-determined activities, I am still able to enjoy myself. I plan to go on more trips in the future.

The Visits Continue

The Omnimax Theater, Saint Louis Science Center was one of the places we visited.

Another was the Palace Theater.

Highland, Illinois

The map(s) details the vast area where we visited during our tours.

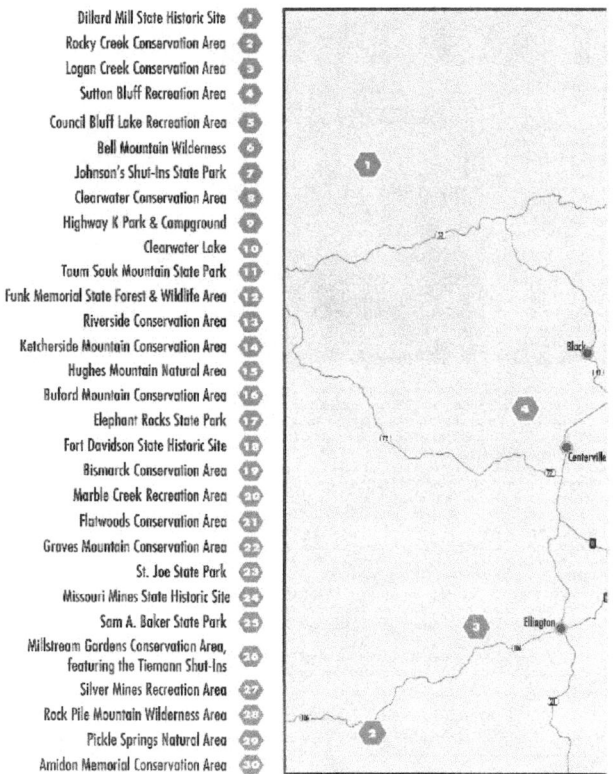

- Dillard Mill State Historic Site (1)
- Rocky Creek Conservation Area (2)
- Logan Creek Conservation Area (3)
- Sutton Bluff Recreation Area (4)
- Council Bluff Lake Recreation Area (5)
- Bell Mountain Wilderness (6)
- Johnson's Shut-Ins State Park (7)
- Clearwater Conservation Area (8)
- Highway K Park & Campground (9)
- Clearwater Lake (10)
- Taum Sauk Mountain State Park (11)
- Funk Memorial State Forest & Wildlife Area (12)
- Riverside Conservation Area (13)
- Ketcherside Mountain Conservation Area (14)
- Hughes Mountain Natural Area (15)
- Buford Mountain Conservation Area (16)
- Elephant Rocks State Park (17)
- Fort Davidson State Historic Site (18)
- Bismarck Conservation Area (19)
- Marble Creek Recreation Area (20)
- Flatwoods Conservation Area (21)
- Graves Mountain Conservation Area (22)
- St. Joe State Park (23)
- Missouri Mines State Historic Site (24)
- Sam A. Baker State Park (25)
- Millstream Gardens Conservation Area, featuring the Tiemann Shut-Ins (26)
- Silver Mines Recreation Area (27)
- Rock Pile Mountain Wilderness Area (28)
- Pickle Springs Natural Area (29)
- Amidon Memorial Conservation Area (30)

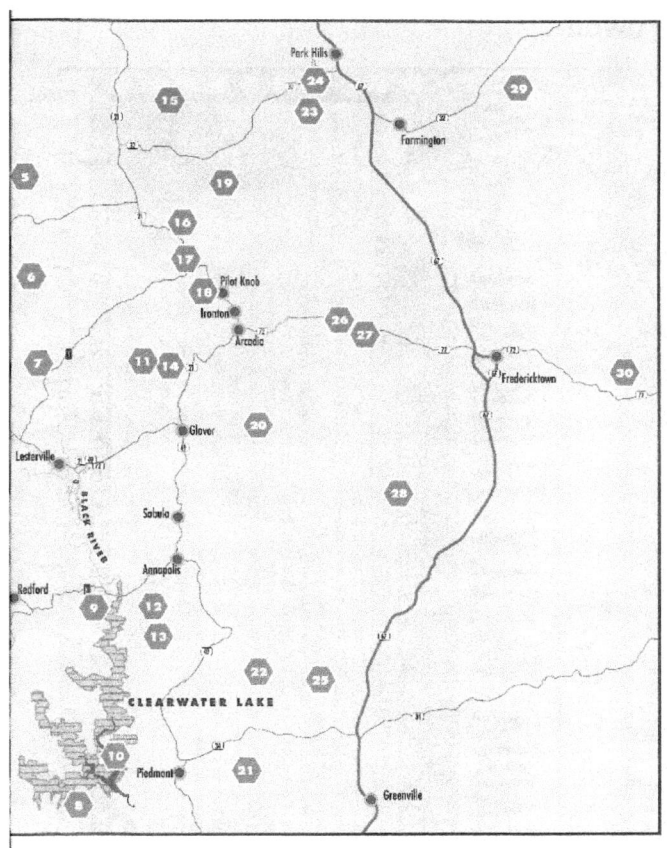

The map of Arcadia Valley was given as compliments of AmerenUE and the businesses in the Arcadia Valley area.

Bobby Powell

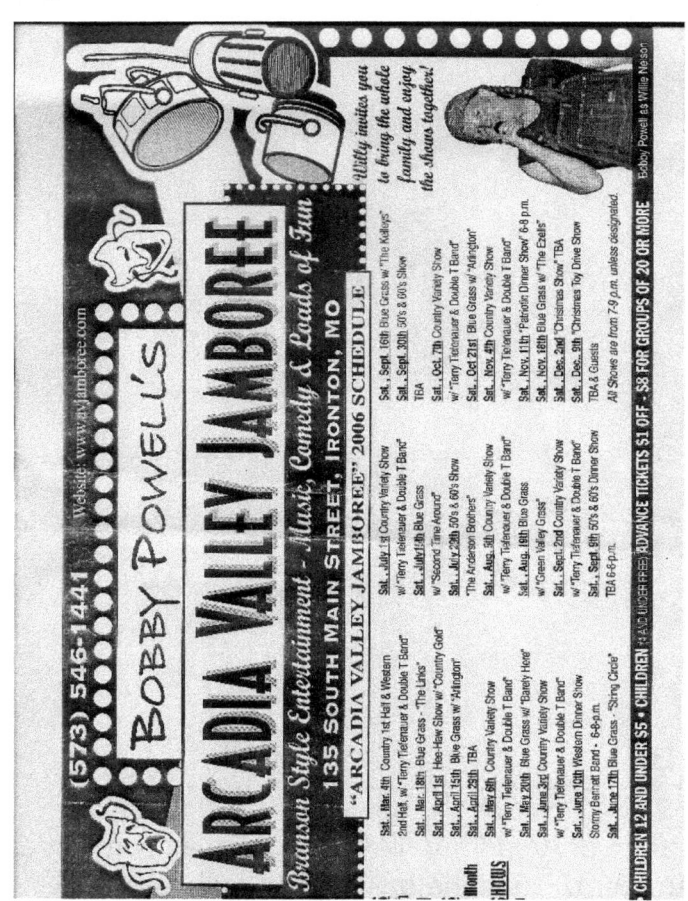

One of our trips was to Ironton, Missouri for music, comedy and fun.

Jefferson City, Missouri

Crown Valley Winery

Crown Valley Events
All bands play from 2 - 6 p.m. unless listed otherwise.

Saturday, October 18
Live Music - Dr. Zhivegas

Sunday, October 19
Live Music - Just Mr.

Saturday, October 25
Live Music - Doc Rocks Party Band

Sunday, October 26
Live Music - Contagious

Saturday, November 1 (1-5 p.m.)
Live Music - Dave Caputo

Sunday, November 2 (1-5 p.m.)
Live Music - Scott Laytham & Karl "Trickee" Holmes

Saturday, November 8 (1-5 p.m.)
Winemaker's Weekend
Live Music - Tiny Crows

Sunday, November 9 (1-5 p.m.)
Winemaker's Weekend
Live Music - Cbox Prophets

Saturday, November 29 (1-5 p.m.)
Thanksgiving Weekend
Live Music - Dave & Greg Show

Information On Crown Country's New Year's Gala Coming Soon. Visit www.crownvalleywinery.com For Upcoming Events.

Online Personalized Labeling System
www.crownvalleywinery.com

Select a label, Personalize your message and Choose a wine.

Easy as 1, 2, 3!

Crown Valley Winery - 23589 State Route WW - Ste. Genevieve, MO 63670
p. 866-207-9463

Crown Valley Winery

Crown Valley Winery (Missouri)

Crown Country

About Your Visit

Ulysses S. Grant National Historic Site is located at 7400 Grant Road in south St. Louis County, just off Gravois Road (Hwy 30) and adjacent to Anheuser-Busch's Grant's Farm. The park is open daily from 9 a.m. to 5 p.m., except Thanksgiving Day, December 25, and January 1. Admission is free.

The visitor center offers an information desk, sales area, exhibits, theater, restrooms, and park offices. The site's historic structures display a variety of interpretive exhibits. Free visits inside the historic home are offered on a ticketed basis, and additional interpretive programs are presented throughout the year. Junior Ranger activities are available for children. Groups of 15 or more require reservations; please call (314) 842-3298 for additional information.

Accessibility
Most areas within the park are wheelchair-accessible.

More Information
Ulysses S. Grant National Historic Site
7400 Grant Road
St. Louis, MO 63123
www.nps.gov/ulsg

Ulysses S. Grant National Historic Site is one of over 380 parks in the National Park System. The National Park Service cares for these special places saved by the American people so that all may experience our heritage. Visit www.nps.gov to learn more about parks and National Park Service programs in America's communities.

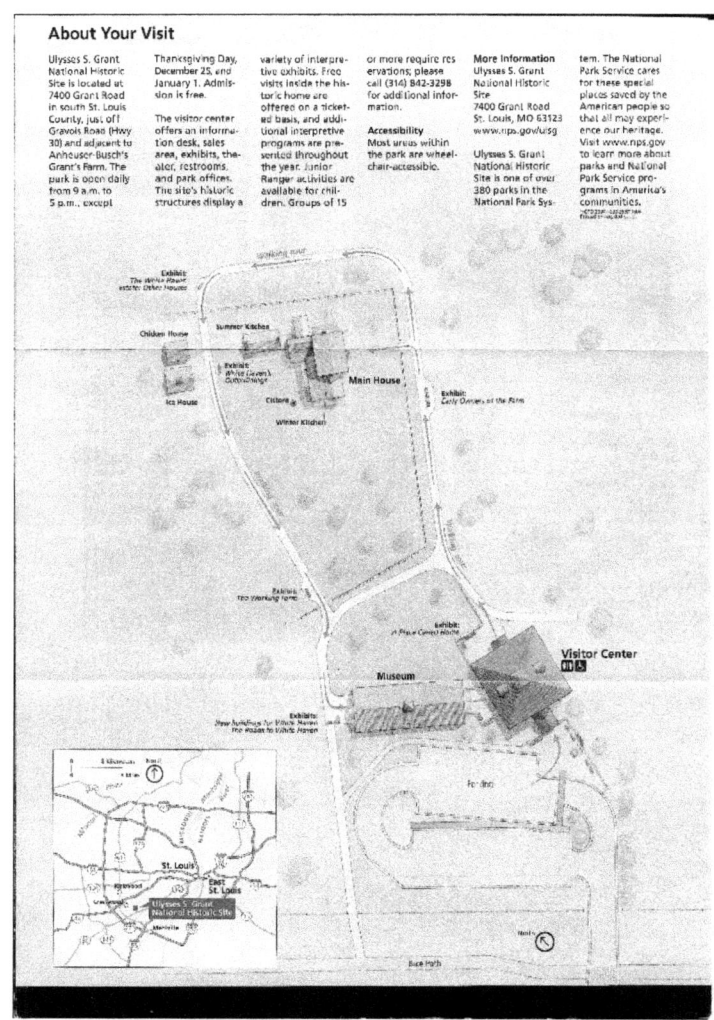

Growing Old and Being All Alone

When you're young, you don't think about these things, but it happens to everyone. If you live a long time, this will definitely happen to you. If you don't have any children, and no one living in your family around, this is what you will have to deal with.

If you mistreat people, then they will not even want to remember you. Life is a gift. If you don't take care of your life, you won't be remembered.

Mayfair Hotel, St. Louis (Public Domain photo)

In this walk of life, treat yourself and others right. Never forget about the people who were nice to you. Always count your blessings. Keep yourself safe and remember that everyone wants to be remembered. You want people to say good things about you when you're gone.

This reminds me of our visit to Grant's Farm in St. Louis and the history behind it and the story of Ulysses S. Grant and his family.

One day when you are free, visit the Ulysses S. Grant National Historic Site in Missouri, Anheuser

Busch Brewery and Grant's Farm. All the history of slavery is there.

A Precious Thing

A fixture can be a pin that passes down from generation to generation. It's only important to you and no one else. A Fixture can be a frame wrapped in a towel placed in a box, put aside for a few years. You start to think about it and you open it up. You look at it and it brings back memories that are important to you and no one else.

It's funny how little things can mean so much to you. I remember when my boyfriend bought me a box of chocolate for Valentine's Day. It meant the world to me. When he had more money, he bought heart-shaped boxes, but I think about the plain box sometimes.

People think that the more money spent on a person, the more the gift-giver loves the receiver. I knew a person who loved a girl so much, but he didn't have enough money for a ring. So he bought a ring in a vending machine. Everyone called him "cheap." But the girl loved the ring and a year later, as finances, they bought a diamond ring. Now both rings are in her jewelry box.

People ask her why she didn't throw the fake ring away. She said that it was the thought that counted. People just shake their heads because they don't get it.

Money isn't everything. It's who you are and what's important to you. I'm not saying that we don't need money, but little things are just as important as big things. What matters is what you're giving from the heart.

St. Louis Art Museum (usage by written permission) "Power and Glory: Court Arts of China's Ming Dynasty" (Image ©David Ulmer)

During one of the trips I saw "Power and Glory" Court Arts of China's Ming Dynasty: 10:00 A.M. tour time at the Saint Louis Art Museum – Forest Park- St. Louis (MO); Wednesday March 4, 2009.

The Saint Louis Science Center

We visited the Saint Louis Science Center and saw several displays:

1) MacGillivray Freeman's - The Alps - A true-life story of a climber attempts to scale the legendary mountain that took his father's life.
2) Mummies: Secrets of the Pharaohs in the Omnimax Theater (Science Center)
3) Tombs of the great pharaohs of Egypt; secrets behind the mummification process and its role in ancient society – a group of scientists unwrap the secrets of the pharaohs

WITTMOND HOTEL
BRUSSELS, IL 62013
618-883-2345

Historic Wittmond Hotel began operation in as a trading post built by Conrad and Mary Wittmond in 1847. The general store sold dry goods, furnishings, livery items, clothing and all other goods that pioneer family might need. With the rapid growth of the Riverboat trade after the Civil War, the family saw a need to provide accommodations to river travelers. In 1863, the Wittmond's constructed the two story brick house that formerly housed the Brussels Post Office, on the West side of the store. In 1885, they rebuilt the current hotel structure, adding 15 rooms for overnight guests.

Whittmond Hotel

```
SHE    708681              THE SHELDON PRESENTS
SHE2CC09B                  ST. LOUIS RAGTIMERS
07/16/2009
   ORCH CENTER                    * * *
   CPEIMANN
   CENTER                  THE SHELDON CONCERT HALL
                           3648 WASHINGTON BLVD.
   G        0.00
   N        9.60      WED NOV 11, 2009 10AM

   6        0.00      CENTER   N    6    9.60
```

Breakfast and a Movie

Have a delicious breakfast at the St. Louis Science Center. Then, see The Alps by MacGillivray Freeman. This is a true story about the climb of the Eiger by the mountaineer and journalist, John Harlin III.

  Date: Thursday, July 10, 2008

  Cost: $30 covers transportation, breakfast and movie

  Depart: Leave the Centre at 7:45 AM

Breakfast is at 8:45 AM. The movie is at 10:00 AM.

Contact Maryland Heights Centre to sign up for the trip or for more information (314) 434-1919.

This was how I got involved in St. Louis traveling.

Mr.   Ms.   Mrs.

Name: _____
Address: _____
City: _____
State: _____ Zip: _____
Birthday: Mo: _____ Day: _____
Anniversary Month _____
Is this your first visit?
  ☐ Yes ☐ No
E-Mail (please write legibly)
Una Cosa Rara (Play)
How did you hear about us?
Una Cosa Rara
Play
Comments: _____
_____
_____
Server_____ Date_6-6-08_

Highway 61 Roadhouse & Kitchen

Bevo Mill Restaurant, St. Louis, MO public domain photo

The History of Bevo Mill

During the years prior to Europe's involvement in World War I, August A. Busch, Sr. and his architects explored the Old World for examples of Flemish architectural styles with the intention of building an authentic windmill in St. Louis.

When Busch returned to St. Louis, he chose the spot, in 1915, at Gravois Road and Morganford because it was approximately halfway between the Anheuser Busch Brewery and Grant's Farm, his home.

Mr. Busch used the beautiful Mill Room as his private dining room for many years. The remainder of the restaurant was opened to the public in 1917 and carried out Mr. Busch's idea of a constructive temperance policy. Back when prohibition was the controversy of the day, the Bevo Mill served only Bevo, (a non-alcoholic drink that tasted like beer), regular beer and wines to its clientele. The drinks were served only at tables, usually with meals. A novel idea back then, the practice became very popular and resulted in the Bevo becoming a favorite family restaurant.

Completed in 1916 for the then-incredible sum of $250,000, the Bevo boast quite a few unique architectural details. The exterior of the building is finished with stones personally gathered by Mr. Busch from Grant's Farm. Following the German and Dutch traditions, a pair of storks are mounted on top of the chimney to ensure good luck.

The vaulted ceilings of the foyer and Mill Room have groined arches which end in stone-carved gnomes, originally exhibited at the Paris exposition of 1889. All tiles, light fixtures and millwork are original, carefully restored through 1984-1986.

The Brewery spent 20 months and over one million dollars to renovate the Bevo. We take great pleasure in recreating the old traditions and adding some new traditions for your dining pleasure.

*This house is not handicap accessible.

All proceeds from the Victorian Christmas Celebration will benefit the projects and programs of the Junior League of Peoria.

The Ballance-Herschel House in Peoria's historic Randolph-Roanoke neighborhood is a beautifully maintained home easily located off I-74 near downtown Peoria, Illinois.

The Ballance-Herschel House was built in 1888 by Willis H. Ballance, Sr. Willis was the son of Col. Charles Ballance, a pioneer Peorian, who settled here in 1831 to practice law.

Upon Willis Ballance's death in 1913, the house was sold to Paul E. Herschel, Sr. of the Herschel Manufacturing Company, makers of agricultural implements.

In 1979, the Junior League of Peoria purchased the Ballance-Herschel House

Victorian Christmas Celebration Purpose

Benefiting the projects and programs
of the Junior League of Peoria

Home Tours – December 5th 5:00-7:00pm
Tickets $5 in advance, $10 at the door

Victorian Tea – December 5th 11:00 & 2:00
Tickets $18 in advance only

Christmas Marketplace – December 5th
Open during all other events

256 Northeast Randolph Avenue
Peoria, IL 61606
(309) 685-9312
www.juniorleagueofpeoria.org

JUNIOR LEAGUE OF PEORIA
Women building better communities

Victorian Christmas

Wasting Away

I get tired of people telling sick people lies when they lose weight, because they are sick. In the sick person's face, people say, "You look great!" But behind their back, they say the opposite. Who cares! It's your body. You may be broken down, but you're still in there.

People can't accept what happens when others begin to change. Don't fall into self-loathing. If you do, that's your problem. Children who are dealt a bad hand, deal with their problems.

There are programs to help them. You have two choices: cry about your problems, or enjoy your life.

You're not at the worst possible thing. You could be dead. Get out. Go for a walk. Talk to the garbage man. Take a long bath.

Give your body the rest it deserves. Your body took care of you. Don't turn on it because it let you down. If you didn't take care of yourself, why are you mad at people when they talk about you being sick? You did not take care of your feet when they were hurting when you could walk. Now you're in a wheelchair, and you're upset about it. Well, at least your feet are getting rest now.

If you don't take care of something, it will eventually fall apart. Listen to your body when it gives you a signal. Ignoring your body comes with too high of a price. In the end, you're supposed to think about yourself. You only have one life and one body. Stop looking negatively at yourself. It is important that you don't lose sight of that.

Don't be so negative about your skin changes. Just take care of your body and your inner spirit. **LOVE YOURSELF!**

Crush

A group of us was talking about when we were young and about how our minds were as children. We discussed crushes, whether it be a doctor, teacher, or a movie star. In our minds, they were handsome, cute, or beautiful. We never thought about them becoming old.

Just like they changed, so did we. Some became bald, fat, out of shape, or even sick. But in a child's eye, you only see the current person.

When you have a crush, you dream about them. The good thing about crushes is that they don't last forever. It only lasts as a child.

Sometimes you become disappointed when you find out how these people really look. A crush is what you carry in your heart, your dream; no one else's.

Boxes

The Story of Boxes

The 1st box is full of baby rattles, bottles, sip cups, baby shoes, and baby pictures.

The 2nd box is full of hair ribbons, dolls, stuffed pink rabbits with orange carrots.

The 3rd box is full of your first lost tooth, and the money from the tooth fairy.

The 4th box is full of jacks and marble games.

The 5th box is full of photos of your first boy/girlfriend, and the first movie ticket.

The 6th box is full of the eighth-grade certificate.

The 7th box is full of disappointments, memories of moving and/or losing your boy/girlfriend.

The 8th box is full of memories of graduation and young adulthood.

The 9th box is full of your work stubs, and memories of hard work.

The 10th box is full of false teeth, dentures, glasses, prescriptions, wrinkles, and worry.

The 11th box is full of wigs and hair pieces, and memories of hair falling out little by little.

The 12th box is empty. I'm too tired to put anything in it.

If you want these boxes, you can have them. I have no more use for them.

Sparkles

Sometimes I wonder what sparkles mean to people. Could it be a first look in the eye, or a feeling after the birth of your first child; or the feeling of your first kiss?

Could it be a crystal glass that sparkles with a shine? A new pair of glasses? When the moon captures your eye and you can stare at it all night? Can it be a diamond?

Well, as time goes by, sparkles are harder to find because things are no longer a mystery.

Are your eyes playing a trick on you? All you see is what you want to see – something that captures your eye. Well, being remembered in the eyes of others as a sparkle must be a mystery. Remember your eyes play tricks on you.

Window Of Yourself

It amazes me how people talk about their loved ones. If you think a family member is cute, keep it to yourself because to the world, that individual may be unattractive (not only considering their physical features, but their attitudes and personalities too).

You can't force your opinion about a family member on the world. Even though you love them, you think higher of them because they are your family

It's always someone you want, but who doesn't want you. You have to appreciate life before you can love someone. There is no need to always argue. If you love someone, you love the whole package, including their faults.

Some people never find love because they are trying to find themselves. You aren't going to find yourself in another person because you aren't perfect.

If you like being lonely, then don't complain about your life. If you alienate everyone by arguing with them, eventually you will have no company and you will begin to mutter to yourself.

Then how will you feel? You still have your family, but as you can probably see, family dies too. But when you're lonely, you never have anyone but yourself.

Listen to your mind, not your heart. Sure, you may have been hurt, but you will get over it in time.

Window

Damage

I used to hear people say, "You can't save damage from damage."

I've found that to be very true. I see people trying to fix other persons, who never become fixed. Let me explain it this way. You break a cup and you put it back together, but the crack is still there. It will never be the same cup again. This is what happens to broken people. You can't fix people, even though they may be just like you.

You can't see the cracks inside of people. You can nurse the outside of a person, but you can't heal the wound on the inside. Sometimes you have to know when to let go because eventually you'll be the next one damaged.

Never regret letting a damaged person go because you tried. It's not your fault. Look and see where your life is.

Search For Truth

Have you ever wondered who you are? I'm not talking about your race or gender? I'm talking about the person inside of you. Why do people feel that they have to lie about everything?

Does it make you feel good about yourself when you realize you have no feeling? Is it a cold heart or no worries? Does it feel good to lie on family members or peers…? I don't get it

Why do others have to suffer from your lies? Once you put it out there it will never return. We are taught not to lie as a child, but we grow up to lie.

I really don't understand. People are so quick to believe lies instead of the truth. Is it because the truth is not as exciting? I don't understand. I throw my hands up.

Publicdomainpictures.net

Thrown Away

When you think of thrown away, you think of trash. Every day, someone is being thrown away. Young people are classified as bad news. But when they grow up, you need their vote to put someone in office, and then they are important. You talk about how teenagers have no respect, but you have to have respect in order to give it.

These children become adults and they never forget about how they were treated. That's why they don't care about their elders as adults. Then you have the senior citizens. As adults, they played by all the rules. They went to work every day. They even paid their taxes. As soon as they turned older, they asked for crumbs. They may be fired from their low paying, part-time job. Or if they become sick, they eventually get put out of the hospital.

Then you have the homeless and the children. These people need care, but since they can't take care of themselves, and can't pay, doctors don't want to help them. They have no health insurance, and they are sick.

Time goes by and eventually the homeless is put in an institution or jail. And since the baby has a parent who doesn't know how to love, the cycle of crime continues.

I remember when people used to care about each other. Now they feel that they have no reason to believe in anything. This is why I wrote this, so thrown away has a new meaning.

I hope there is someone who cares because the voice of the homeless is dying out, and becoming silenced. Who will speak for the thrown away? People don't realize that everyone matters. Everything isn't about material things. It's caring for the sick, and those who can't speak for themselves.

Life's Changing
In Front Of Your Eyes

You realize that you're only in your twenties and that you're unhappy. You can't go back to your teenage years because time goes on and your old friends don't even remember you. You are strangers again.

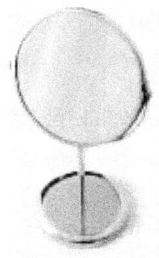

People even pretend that they don't remember how they mistreated you. I realize that I've made plenty of mistakes, and those mistakes have all taught me something. I can barely remember my thirties.

But in my twenties, I had my first crisis when my first-born and I were at my cousin's house. We had left the door open and my two-year old child walked out of the house and down the street. We had to stop him from crossing the street when a bus was coming his way.

My second crisis was when he found my mother's pills without a childproof top. He swallowed some of them. I had to put my finger down his throat so that he would throw them up. Then I called the hospital and they told me not to let him sleep.

We walked around the neighborhood for four hours. I was not going to let him sleep. That was my last crisis with that child.

My second born was another story. When he was sweeping the porch, broken glass got in his chin. He had to get stiches. Then he choked on lemon drops.

The next crisis involved me when I was having an asthma attack. The children did not know what to do. I had to catch my breath on my own.

Finally, my children were getting older. I had two sons. One was 12 and the other 9. However, after my attack, their sister had a crisis. She was six years old. She woke up staring in space. I called her name … no reply. I realized that she was losing body fluid. I called an ambulance, but the response was not prompt. So I asked my older son and friend to help me.

When the ambulance finally arrived, technicians put equipment in her mouth. Later on, they said that she had a seizure. She woke up and didn't remember anything. However, she had her family, and that's what mattered.

The next crisis was when my second child had an asthma attack due to an allergic reaction. We finally found the item that caused the reaction. He wasn't able to play outside as much. He just had to be really careful.

When you're a mother, you never know what's going to happen next. For a while, nothing happened, but the next crisis was around the corner when we moved into a new house. My youngest child found the hiding place for our key. She walked out of the house and walked down the sidewalk right by cars and traffic. I found her and the first thing that I thought was that if someone found her, they would ask where I was.

I took her into the house, calmed down and found another place to hide the key. When she turned three, she had her hair braded with beads. She stuck the beads up her nose. I made her smell black pepper and she sneezed them out. She never got her hair braided with beads again.

As the children were getting older, I thought that the crisis was over, but I was wrong. My sons were long gone out of the house, and on their own. It was just me, my husband, and my daughters. My husband said he wasn't feeling well. So we made a doctor's appointment. He was scheduled for the next week, but he didn't make it. He was getting worse, so we arranged for a family member to take him to a hospital since I didn't drive. We were right behind him on his way to the hospital.

The doctor walked out of the emergency room telling us that he was in a diabetic coma. I didn't know that he was diabetic. I was all alone. My family left and I went to the parking lot and cried. I asked God not to let him die. I was scared and sick to my stomach. I don't talk to anyone, so I didn't tell him how I felt. That same year I lost my mother. The year later, I lost my father. The worst was yet to come.

I wasn't ready for this crisis, but 2003 – 2004 were my toughest years. I had never been through so much stress. I was going to school as a medical assistant in my fifties. I also changed jobs. I didn't realize that this was too much for my body. I got sick and took a rest for a while.

After that, everything seemed to go well, but for some reason, I started to bloat like a balloon. I would fall asleep a lot too. Doctors examined me and were confused on what was going on.

Finally, doctors realized that I had congestive heart failure. Things changed so fast. I needed help for everything. I even needed physical therapy. I felt like a child instead of an adult. Some people older than me could function better than me.

You don't want pity, but all you do is self-loathe. But then, things got better. I got back on my feet. However, I had lost my job and I wasn't ready for the crisis of 2004 which was my greatest challenge.

My husband's birthday and mine are three weeks apart in different months. Mine is in September, and his in October. When my birthday came, we went to lunch at his favorite restaurant. That was okay with me. When his birthday came around, we were a little short on money, so he went bowling. Three weeks later, he passed.

Everyone was worried about me, but I was alright. I had done my crying in the hospital parking lot in 1992. God had answered my prayers, and gave me more years to spend with him. He was unable to tell me goodbye.
Still I was able to be strong for my children, and I knew that someone was watching over us.

We have been through so much. Even my children's lives changed in front of my eyes. We have seen so much pain and sorrow. Some people have been through more than we have, but no one ever gets used to it. Your life is never the same again after a crisis. You try not to feel sorry for yourself, and you try not to let your children know what you are thinking, so you think privately, and hope for the same peace that once filled your home. You pray for a brighter day, and you pray for your children.

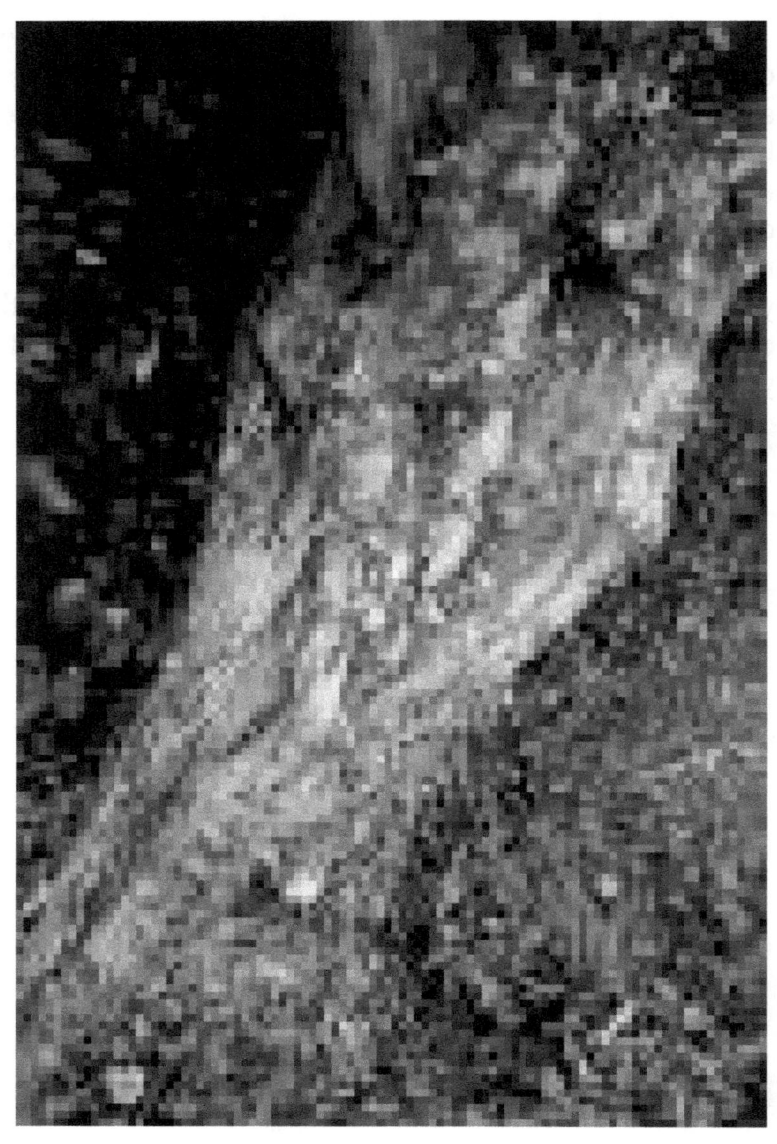
Publicdomainpictures.net

Conclusion: Stop Fighting

Trees and flowers are just like people. They are different, but they know how to live with each other. There are big and small trees and different colored flowers. Yet they all live together.

All of nature lives in harmony. However, it's all different and it all goes against humans, no matter what we do.

A roach can destroy an entire meal just like a fly. Just as nature works together, we need to work together. We need to step up and improve ourselves.

Listen to what I am saying as I give you something to think about. If a tree grows to destroy your pipes, it is nature working together to take back its land. We need to work together, no matter what race. Just like nature is working, you should too. You've been warned, and I hope that you are listening.

Get up. Get involved. Go places.

Dedication

The book is dedicated to all of the children who had a dream and it came true. I also dedicate the book to those who never let their dreams fall by the wayside. (Annette Riley Joseph, St. Louis, MO)

Other Readings and Travels You May Like:

Annette Eloise Riley Joseph

Barry C. Wilkins, artist (MS)

Thanks from the Editor

St. Louis Eads Bridge over the Mississippi River (public domain photo)

Thanks to the artists who shared their pictures through the public domain sites from the internet.

Though not required, we listed you in the credits because you deserve to be known.

The advice in the book is strong and so appropriate for the term of existence in which we live confronting bullying.

The book is age appropriate for all to read.

    From the editor

Suggested travels of places I visited:

St. Louis Ragtimers

Formed in 1961, the St. Louis Ragtimers combine the folk rags of Missouri and the stomps and shouts of New Orleans to create a unique style that could be performed on St. Louis riverboats. From the 1960s – 1980s the group called the Goldenrod Showboat home, hosting a jazz and ragtime festival each summer. To continue their Dixieland legacy, they have traveled to various festivals around the world, created more than half a dozen albums, and been featured on NBC's *Today Show*. Featuring Trebor Tichenor on piano, Al Striker on banjo, Don Franz on tuba, and Phil Mason on cornet, the St. Louis Ragtimers perform a dynamic style of ragtime and Dixieland jazz that is sure to get your toes tappin'.

Trebor Tichenor, the band's leader, has created an international reputation for himself as a ragtime pianist and composer. He currently teaches the history of ragtime music at Washington University. Known for his research, Tichenor boasts a collection of piano rolls, sheet music and rare recordings. He has recorded six solo albums and co-authored *Rags and Ragtimes*, with David Jansen. Tichenor has been awarded many honors, including the Scott Joplin Foundation Award for "extraordinary contributions to the field of ragtime" in 1992.

Jefferson Landing State Historic Site and Missouri State Museum

Missouri Department of Natural Resources

Mr.   Ms.   Mrs.

Name: _____
Address: _____
City: _____
State: _____ Zip: _____
Birthday: Mo: _____ Day: _____
Anniversary Month_____
Is this your first visit?
      ▢ Yes   ▢ No
E-Mail (please write legibly)
Una Casa Rara (Play)
How did you hear about us?
Una Casa Rara Play
Comments:_____
_____
_____
Server_____ Date 6-6-08

CROWN VALLEY WINERY

Missouri's Premier Winery

Moonlight Restaurant, Inc.
3400 Fosterburg Road
Alton, IL 62002

Since 1937
We are located 1 mile north of
Route 140 on Fosterburg Road

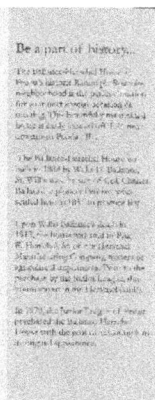

Food & Drinks including Crown Valley Wine Tastings
Live entertainment
Local arts & crafts
Tiger viewing all day
Raffles & auctions throughout the weekend

Billy Kaufmann 11/9/1980 - 5/14/2007

This year's Fall Festival will promote bike awareness and will be in honor of our friend Billy Kaufmann.
On May 14, 2007, as Billy Kaufmann was riding his motorcycle home from work, he was struck and killed by a reckless driver. Join us for the Fall Festival to honor Billy's memory by raising awareness of the need for others to share the road with bikers & cyclists.

To make your reservation please call 573.883.9909. Reservations are not required, but are appreciated. The first 25 people to make a reservation will receive a free gift bag! Proceeds will help support our tigers like Mohan, our white tiger.

Crown Ridge Exhibit

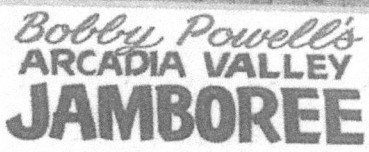

Bobby Powell's ARCADIA VALLEY JAMBOREE

135 South Main, Ironton, MO 63650
www.avjamboree.com
www.arcadiavalley.biz • (573) 546-1441
Showtimes 7 - 9 PM

Country Variety Shows
1st Saturday of the Month
February thru December

Bluegrass Shows
3rd Saturday of the Month
February thru November

50's - 60's Shows
5th Saturday of the Month
February thru November

Dinner Shows - By Reservation Only
Watch Our Website or Call For Details,
Prices, and Additional Shows

Legends Show • Feb. - Valentine's Day
Western Show • 2nd Sat. of June
50's - 60's Show • 2nd Sat. of Sept.
Patriotic Show • 2nd Sat. of Nov.
Christmas Shows • 1st & 2nd Sat. of Dec.
Additional Shows & Matinees
May Be Added By Request

Trip to Jefferson City

Travel with Maryland Heights Parks and Recreation to tour the Governor's Mansion and Capitol Building in the morning. Then, lunch at the Prison Brews. After lunch, take a tour of the State Penitentiary. Before leaving Jefferson City, we will stop at Central Dairy for a small ice cream cone.

Date: Tuesday, June 15, 2010
Time: Bus leaves the Centre at 7:30 am
Cost: $55 covers transportation, admissions, lunch, ice cream treat, tax and gratuity.

Sign up at the Maryland Heights Centre (314) 738-2599. Plan on a long day.

MISSOURI STATE PENITENTIARY
through the years

1831 — Governor John Miller suggested a prison be built in Jefferson City to help ensure the city remained the seat of Missouri government.

1833 — January 3, the Missouri House of Representatives passed a bill (25-24) to establish and build a penitentiary in Jefferson City, the Missouri State Penitentiary (MSP).

1834 — Construction began on the first state prison west of the Mississippi River.

1836 — Wilson Eidson, MSP's first inmate, arrived from Greene County.

1842 — In May, the first female inmate, Amelia Eddy, arrived from St. Louis County.

1885 — Six major shoe factories and numerous other industries, including the largest saddletree factory in the world, contribute to the Jefferson City economy utilizing inmate labor.

1893 — MSP is considered one of the most efficient prisons in the country, housing and feeding inmates for $0.11 per day.

1900 — The Jefferson City Star Tribune declared the Missouri Penitentiary the "Greatest in the World." By then, an average of 2,200 convicts lived behind the walls.

1911 — February 5. MSP convicts save thousands of documents when the Missouri State Capitol is destroyed by fire.

1922 Inmate Harry Snodgrass gained the title of "The Most Popular Radio Entertainer." He was known as "King of the Ivories" in his radio broadcast from the dome of the capitol building.

Charles Arthur "Pretty Boy" Floyd arrives at MSP. **1925**

MSP becomes the largest prison in the United States with 5,200 inmates. **1932**

Missouri Gas Chamber constructed by inmates. It would be the location of 40 executions. **1937**

1954 A major riot occured focusing national attention on MSP.

1967 MSP is called "The bloodiest 47 acres in America" by a national magazine.

1991 The name is changed from Missouri State Penitentiary to the Jefferson City Correctional Center. (JCCC)

Groundbreaking for the new JCCC takes place and the name of the old institution is changed back to Missouri State Penitentiary. **2001**

Wednesday, September 15. 1,355 inmates are moved from the Missouri State Penitentiary to the Jefferson City Correctional Center. The Missouri State Penitentiary served Missouri as the oldest prison west of the Mississippi River for over 168 years. **2004**

2009 May 2. MSP opened its doors to the public for hard hat tours.

Photos courtesy of Missouri State Archives and Stephen Brooks.

gas chamber

Pere Marquette Lodge napkin

City of MARYLAND HEIGHTS

Parks and Recreation
2344 McKelvey Road
Maryland Heights, MO 63043-1632
t: 314.738.2599 f: 314.738.2590
www.marylandheights.com

May 26, 2010

Annette Joseph
2369 Wesford
Maryland Heights, MO 63043

Re: Jefferson City trip

Dear Annette:

Thank you for travelling with Maryland Heights Parks and Recreation to Jefferson City.

We leave the Centre on June 15th at 7:30 am. We will take a rest stop around 8:30 am and finish the trip around 9:45 am. Our first tour will be at the Governor's Mansion at 10am. We can take pictures, however, no flash is permitted. There are no restroom facilities at the Mansion. We would be able to use the facilities at the Governor offices at the corner of Madison Street and Capitol Avenue.

We walk to the Capitol Building for an 11:00 am tour (map enclosed). There are restroom facilities on the first floor of the Capitol Building. The tour is about an hour long.

We leave for the restaurant, Prison Brews, for lunch. Beer sampling in shot glasses will be offered. After lunch, we leave at 1:30 pm for the tour of the State Penitentiary. They only have port-a-potties at the prison. Please use the facilities at the restaurant before we leave for the prison. Enclosed is a menu for you to choose your lunch. Please complete and return it to me by June 4th.

The final tour for the day is the Missouri State Penitentiary. The steel gate will clank behind you just like it did with inmates entering the prison. You will tour the upper yard, then take a seat in the oldest housing unit from 1868. You will hear history and stories of the inmates, explore the cells and walk through the front entrance to the bus. The bus will drive around the block to the lower level to the gas

Association letter for traveling itinerary

Places Visited

Alan Dale Brew
314-870-0473
nailedpiknjed@hotmail.com
August 8, 2007
Maryland Heights Center Trip

Aya Sofia Turkish/Mediterranean Cuisine Restaurant
March 19, 2007
314-645-9919
314-645-9920

The Balance-Herschel House, 256 N.E. Randolph,
Peoria (Illinois)
juniorleagueofpeoria.org
Guests comment about the trip and meal
Market Place
309-685-9312

Bevo Mill Restaurant, St. Louis (MO) opened to the
public in 1917
www.bemillst.com
www.budweisertour.com
Marta Spiros Gift Cards
314-838-3594
314-577-2626
Collection Name: Commerce and Industrial Development Collection
Photographer/Studio: Massie, Gerald R.

Description: Windmill outside Bevo Mill Restaurant in South St. Louis City.
Coverage: United States – Missouri – St. Louis City
Date: 1955
Rights: Copyright is in the public domain.
Credit: Courtesy of Missouri State Archives
Image Number: CID_051_035
Institution: Missouri State Archives

**Bobby Powell's
Arcadia Valley**
Jamboree
9/27/2006
www.avjamboree.com

**Cicero
www.ciceros-stl.com**

Crown Ridge Tiger Sanctuary
19620 State Route B
Ste. Genevieve, Missouri 65670
573-883-9909
www.crownridge.com

Eckert's Orchards, Belleville (Illinois) – Pick-Your-Own

Eckert's Country Store & Farms – Fun-Country Style

Eckert's Country Restaurant
Belleville, Illinois
www.Eckerts.com
peach and apple trip (April 19, 2010)
618-233-0513, ext. 3
951 Green Mount Road
Belleville, Illinois 62220
www.Eckert.com
Maryland Heights Center Trip

Fairmont Park
9301 Collinsville Road
Collinsville, Illinois
FairmontPark.com
For Horse Race   Fax 618-346-1051
itboffp@wisperhome.com
May 9, 2009 – August 28, 2012

The Fountain on Locust – A restaurant – St. Louis (MO)

The Full Monty Stages
The Robert G. Reim Theatre
P.O. Box 220012
St. Louis, MO 63122

The Highland House of Plenty (11/8/2006)

Jefferson City, Missouri State Capitol

Jefferson Landing State Historic Site and Missouri State Museum, Jefferson City, Missouri, Room B-2
State Capitol 65101
573-751-2854
800-334-6946
April 19, 2010

Maryland Heights Parks and Recreation Centre

The Mayfair (A Wyndham Historic Hotel), St. Louis, Missouri

MetroTix – Power and Glory: Court, Arts of China's Ming Dynasty (St. Louis Art Museum), 2009

Miss Aimee B's Tea Room & The Upstairs Market Place, St. Charles (Missouri)

Missouri Department of Natural Resources Riverboat Cruises
gatewayarch.com
877-982-1410

Missouri State Capitol
Jefferson City, Missouri 65101
June 15, 2010
573-751-2854

Missouri State Penitentiary (Jefferson City, MO, 2007)
Photo courtesy of Missouri State Archives and Stephen Brooks
June 15, 2010
573-635-0678
Jefferson City Convention and Visitors' Bureau
100 East High Street
Jefferson City, Missouri
Attention: Prison Tours

Missouri State Penitentiary Gas Chamber, Jefferson City (MO) 1836-2004

Moonlight Restaurant, Inc., 3400 Fosterburg Road, Alton (Illinois) – catering and banquet services
www.moonlightrestaurant.com

The Palace Theatre, owned by Dennis and Mary Lou Ammann of Highland, Illinois (9/27/2006)

Par-A-Dice
Peoria, Illinois (dinner buffet) Casino

Pere Marquette Lodge (Grafton, Illinois), September 4, 2008
www.PMLodge.net

Prison Brews Brewery-Restaurant-Bocce
(established 2008),
305 Ash Street
Jefferson City (MO) 65101
June 15, 2010

Puccini La Boheme Opera Translations
http://www.bohemianopers.com/ariahtm

Repertory Theatre of St. Louis
"Sleuth"
130 Edgar Road
P.O. Box 191730
St. Louis, Missouri 63119
314-968-4925
Maryland Heights Center Trip

Riverboat Cruises

Roberts' Bistro - formerly Mayfair Hotel (11/7/2008)

Roberts' Orpheum Theater/Old American Theatre (8/25/2008)

Saint Charles Tour of the historical Miss Aimee B, (April/26/2008)
www.missaimeeb.com

Saint Louis Art Museum
March 1, 2009 – Court Art of China Ming Dynasty
Photo permission usage from Art Museum February 7, 2015
Photo permission usage from photographer

St. Louis Ragtimers at the Sheldon Concert Hall, 3648 Washington Boulevard in St. Louis (MO) 2009

Saint Louis Science Center
Breakfast & More
(Secret of the Pharaohs) 3/19/2007 and July 10, 2008
The Alps by McGillivray
1-800-456-SHCC x 4424 or 314-289-4424
slsc.org (April 10, 2008

The Sheldon Art Galleries
3648 Washington Boulevard
St. Louis, Missouri 63108
November 11, 2009
www.thesheldon.org

Sheldon Coffee Corner
July 29, 2009
Ragtime, lunch, chat, fountain, band

Ulysses S. Grant National Historic Site, dedicated to Civil War General and 18th President Ulysses S. Grant and his wife Julia Dent Grant (South St. Louis County, Missouri) 7400 Grant Road, St. Louis (MO) National Park Service

U.S. Dept. of the Interior
National Historic Site (MO)

Union Avenue Opera
2007 Dress Rehearsal
La Traviata (5/24/2007)
314-961-0644
www.experienceopera.org
(7/30/2010

White Haven and Café Brasil
Ulysses S. Grant/Julia Dent
11/15/2009
314-963-3535

Winding Brook Estate, "A Lavender Farm", Eureka (MO), a 17-acre farm with acres of lavender planted for public harvesting during blooming season – located in the hills of the northern Ozarks in Eureka, Missouri just 20 miles west of St. Louis
04/08/2008

Wittmond Hotel, Brussels (Illinois) 62013
618-888-2345

Wyndham Historic Hotel
314-421-2500) guest rooms

Reference:

U.S. Copyright Office   1-877-476-0778   (2005)
Request copyright certificates.

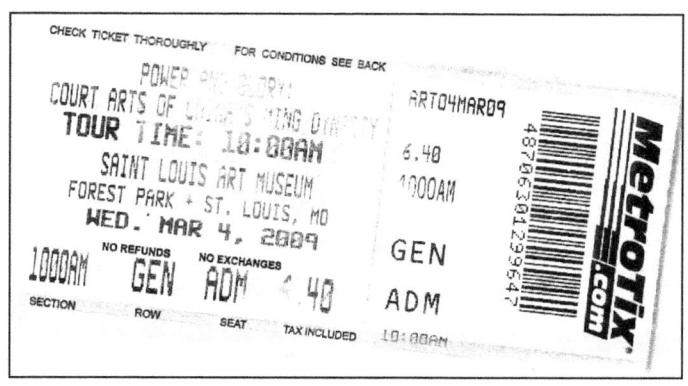

Missouri State Penitentiary (public domain photo)

Missouri State Penitentiary

Jefferson Landing State Historic Site

View of the Jefferson Landing Building, Jefferson City, Cole County, Missouri, by an unknown photographer working for the Historic American Engineering Record. The Jefferson Landing Building is located on the Missouri River close by the Capitol building in Jefferson City. The first section of the building was erected for Richard Shackleford in 1834, then subsequent to 1836 two later additions were constructed for new owner Harry Colgan. The building had many uses through the years, including as a hotel, warehouse, store, and offices for the wharf master. The building later became known as the Lohman's Landing Building after Charles F. Lohman acquired it in 1852.

White Haven, Ulysses S. Grant (slave owner)

Paramount Park (photo by Annette Joseph)

the **Missouri State Capitol**

The Missouri House of Representatives welcomes you to the magnificent State Capitol, considered by many to be one of the most beautiful state houses in the country. ***As our esteemed guest, we don't want you to miss any of the highlights!***

Follow the floor-by-floor STOPS presented in the following pages.

The Capitol covers nearly three acres. It is a symmetrical building of the Roman renaissance style an is situated high atop a bluff overlooking the Missouri River. Completed in 1918, it is the third Capito in Jefferson City's history, and the sixth in Missouri history. Jefferson City's first Capitol burned in 183 and a second structure, completed in 1840 in the same location as the present building, burned whe the dome was struck by lightning in 1911.

Today's Capitol was constructed for $4,215,000, including site and furnishings. It is five stories high 437 feet long, 300 feet wide in the center and 200 feet wide in the wings. The dome, rising 238 fee above ground and topped by a bronze statue of Ceres, goddess of grain, is the first view of Jefferso City for travelers arriving from the north.

The exterior is Missouri's Carthage limestone marble, as are the floors of all corridors, the rotunda and the treads of the stairways. The structure is notable for its architectural features, including it eight 48-foot columns on the south portico and six 40-foot columns on the north side. The gran staircase is 30 feet wide and extends from the front portico to the third floor; it is more than 65 fee from the wall on one side to the wall on the other side. Bronze front doors—each 13 by 18 feet—ar the largest cast since the Roman era.

Statuary is a prominent feature of the Capitol grounds. Heroic bronze figures depicting Missouri's tw great rivers, the Mississippi and the Missouri, flank the south entrance. A 13-foot statue of Thoma Jefferson is the centerpiece of the southern steps. A bronze relief depicting the signing of the Louisi ana Purchase by Livingston, Monroe and Marbois and the Fountain of the Centaurs are outstandin features on the north grounds.

In addition to housing both branches of the legislature, the Capitol provides office space for the gov ernor, state auditor and some administrative agencies.

The Capitol's first floor features the State Museum, which consists of two corridors leading off th rotunda. One corridor is dedicated to Missouri's rich history; the other to Missouri's resources – huma as well as natural. Outstanding paintings, pediments and friezes decorate the Capitol interior.

(cover)

> ### Missouri State Capitol
>
> Missouri" is now a source of pride and a popular stop for visitors touring the Capitol.
>
> Part of the original Capitol plans called for a ground-floor museum that showcased Missouri's cultural and natural history. Now operated by the Missouri Department of Natural Resources, the Missouri State Museum features exhibits, dioramas and changing displays. The east wing of the museum, originally named the Missouri Soldiers and Sailors Memorial Hall in 1919 to recognize Missourians who served during World War I, now serves as the state museum's History Hall. The Resources Museum, created in 1921 to display the products of the state's forests, fields and mines, today serves as the state museum's Resources Hall.
>
> All four floors of Missouri's Capitol are open to the public. A 30-minute guided tour is the best way to experience the historic and decorative features of the building. A walk around the Capitol grounds highlights more of Missouri's history, including Karl Bitter's bronze relief of the signing of the Louisiana Purchase Treaty, which sits on the terrace overlooking the Missouri River.
>
> Whether viewing the interior or exterior, the Missouri state Capitol provides visitors a rewarding glimpse of the cultural and natural legacy of our state.
>
> Missouri State Capitol
> Jefferson City, MO 65101
> 573-751-2854

Cover

I know you enjoyed my suggestions and if you try going places that I just mentioned, then you will not have enough time to deal with anyone else. You will be minding your own damn business.

David Ulmer Photography
404 LaDue
Greenville, IL 62246
314-952-0845 (Power and Glory: Court Arts of China's Ming Dynasty", which was on view at the Saint Louis Art Museum from 02/22/2009 to 05/17/2009. Image ©David Ulmer

    I am telling you about these adventures because, instead of sitting alone at home, feeling sorry for myself, I go out and explore my surroundings. Even though I was too young to join a program with pre-determined activities, I am still able to enjoy myself.

    Enjoy life every day because sometimes life brings many challenges and sometimes you're not prepared for what it throws at you.

"Mind Your Own Damn Business"

Annette Riley Joseph

I am telling you about these adventures because, instead of sitting alone at home, feeling sorry for myself, I go out and explore my surroundings. Even though I was too young to join a program with pre-determined activities, I am still able to enjoy myself.

©2010, 2016

Printed in the United States of America
M.O.R.E. Publishers CO
Memphis, Tennessee

www.ingramcontent.com/pod-product-compliance
Lightning Source LLC
Chambersburg PA
CBHW060817050426
42449CB00008B/1708